J538 FOR
Forest, Christor'
Focus on magr

Guelph I

FEB - - 2018

Hands-On STEM
FOCUS ON MAGNETISM

by Christopher Forest

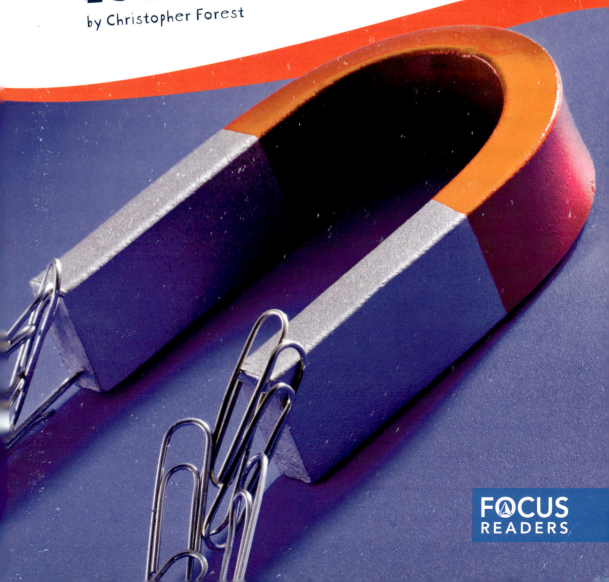

www.focusreaders.com

Copyright © 2018 by Focus Readers, Lake Elmo, MN 55042. All rights reserved. No part of this book may be reproduced or utilized in any form or by any means without written permission from the publisher.

Focus Readers is distributed by North Star Editions:
sales@northstareditions.com | 888-417-0195

Produced for Focus Readers by Red Line Editorial.

Content Consultant: Bruce Bolon, Associate Professor of Physics, Hamline University

Photographs ©: Pat_Hastings/Shutterstock Images, cover, 1; kali9/iStockphoto, 4–5; supersaiyan3/Shutterstock Images, 6; sturti/iStockphoto, 9; lissart/iStockphoto, 10–11; Imgorthand/iStockphoto, 12; PeterHermesFurian/iStockphoto, 14; Red Line Editorial, 17, 27; mactrunk/iStockphoto, 18–19, 29; BanksPhotos/iStockphoto, 21; Hung Chung Chih/Shutterstock Images, 23; kaisersosa67/iStockphoto, 25

ISBN
978-1-63517-285-0 (hardcover)
978-1-63517-350-5 (paperback)
978-1-63517-480-9 (ebook pdf)
978-1-63517-415-1 (hosted ebook)

Library of Congress Control Number: 2017935144

Printed in the United States of America
Mankato, MN
June, 2017

About the Author

Christopher Forest is a middle school teacher. In his free time, he enjoys writing books for all ages. He also enjoys watching sports, playing guitar, reading, and spending time outdoors. He lives in Danvers, Massachusetts, with his wife, Melissa, two children, Brighid and Christopher, and his cat, Murray.

TABLE OF CONTENTS

CHAPTER 1
Attracting and Repelling 5

CHAPTER 2
What Is a Magnet? 11

CHAPTER 3
How Do People Use Magnets? 19

Make a Magnet 26

Focus on Magnetism • 28

Glossary • 30

To Learn More • 31

Index • 32

CHAPTER 1

ATTRACTING AND REPELLING

Jose finishes a drawing that he is very proud of. He wants to put the drawing where his whole family will see it. He holds the drawing against the refrigerator. Then he puts a magnet on top of it.

 Refrigerators are one of the many everyday objects that use magnets.

 Most pins are attracted to magnets.

The magnet clings to the refrigerator. It holds the drawing in place. Why does the magnet stick to the refrigerator? It happens because the refrigerator is made of a magnetic metal. Magnets are **attracted** to these metals. That means magnets are pulled toward them. Not all metals are magnetic. But many are.

Now Jose reaches into a drawer. He grabs two more magnets. He holds the ends close to one another.

But he cannot make the magnets stay together. The ends of the magnets **repel** one other. This means the magnets push apart.

Magnets can either repel or attract. It depends upon how they are lined up. Magnets are an important part of our lives. Many people use them every day.

 A large magnet can pull a small magnet off the table.

CHAPTER 2

WHAT IS A MAGNET?

Humans have been using magnets for thousands of years. In ancient times, people saw that pieces of iron could stick to lodestones. Lodestones are stones that contain iron.

A lodestone attracts a piece of iron.

An electric guitar has strings made of magnetized steel.

Lodestones attract other pieces of iron. They can even magnetize steel. Lodestones may have seemed like magic to ancient people. But over time, scientists learned that lodestones are magnetic.

A magnet is an object that has a magnetic field around it. A magnetic field is invisible. But it may cause nearby objects to feel a force. The magnetic field may push or pull.

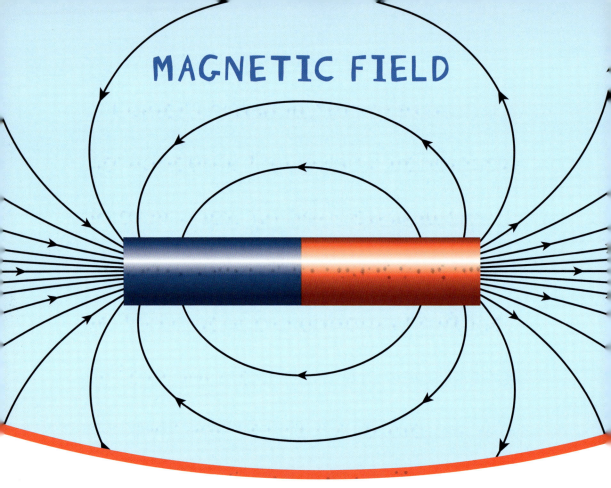

 The magnetic field points in different directions at different locations.

A magnetic field is caused by moving electric charges. **Atoms** are the building blocks of the objects around us. Atoms contain electric charges called **electrons**. These electrons are always in motion. Their motion creates a magnetic field. The magnetic field of one magnet can cause a force on a nearby magnet.

Iron and nickel are two examples of magnetic metals. They are found in many everyday objects. For example, car parts and frying pans are often made of iron. Wires, machines, and coins are often made of nickel.

Magnets have **poles**. Magnetic field lines come out near the magnet's north pole. The lines go in near the magnet's south pole. These field lines never cross.

Magnets can be attracted by other magnets. The north pole of one magnet is attracted to the south pole of another magnet. However, the north pole of one magnet repels the north pole of another magnet. The south poles of two magnets also repel.

MAGNETIC POLES

 Like poles repel, and unlike poles attract.

CHAPTER 3

HOW DO PEOPLE USE MAGNETS?

Magnets have many uses. Sometimes they are used to make objects stay together. This is how a refrigerator door stays closed. One magnet is in the refrigerator. Another magnet is in the door.

Many things in a house use magnets, including computers and tablets.

19

The two magnets are attracted to one another. They cause the door to pull itself shut.

A magnet can also be used to keep objects attached to metal. For example, many schools have magnetic whiteboards. Teachers can attach papers to these boards with magnets.

Some magnets make life easier for workers. Junkyard owners use large machines with powerful magnets on them.

 A powerful magnet is used to move scrap metal at a junkyard.

These machines help them move heavy cars. **Sanitation** companies use magnets when moving trash. Their magnets pull metal out of trash. Then the metal can be recycled. Many computers also rely on magnets. The magnets in a computer help store information.

Magnets can be used for travel, too. For example, some trains have large magnets instead of wheels. The tracks also have magnets. The two magnets repel. So, the train

 Some trains that use magnets can reach speeds of 310 miles per hour (500 km/h).

does not touch the tracks. Instead, the train levitates. Magnetic trains can travel at very high speeds.

People also use magnets to help with directions. Earth has its own magnetic field. That means our planet acts like a giant magnet. A **compass** uses a magnet, too. The magnet points toward one of Earth's poles. This helps people figure out which way to go.

Long ago, magnets seemed like magical objects. But today, they are no longer a mystery. They make life simpler for everyone.

 Compasses can help people who are hiking in the woods.

SCIENCE IN ACTION!

MAKE A MAGNET

What will happen if you rest a steel nail against a magnet? Perform this experiment to find out. Be sure to get help from an adult.

Step 1: Get a screwdriver that is not magnetized. Also get a nail made of steel.

Step 2: Touch the nail to the screwdriver. Watch what happens to the nail.

Step 3: Now get a magnet, and place it on the table.

Step 4: Rest the nail against one end of the magnet. Allow the nail to rest on the magnet for about five minutes.

Step 5: Remove the nail. Place the nail next to the screwdriver again.

A magnetized steel nail is attracted to a screwdriver.

What do you notice? Did the nail behave differently after it rested on the magnet? How can you explain what happened? What would happen if you rested the nail against the magnet for only one minute? What if you rested it for 30 minutes?

FOCUS ON
MAGNETISM

Write your answers on a separate piece of paper.

1. Write a sentence that describes a main idea of Chapter 2.

2. Would your life be more difficult without magnets? Why or why not?

3. What does it mean for an object to be a magnet?
    - **A.** The object is made of metal.
    - **B.** The object has a magnetic field.
    - **C.** The object is made of atoms.

4. Suppose you put the south pole of one magnet near the south pole of another magnet. What would happen?
    - **A.** The magnets will not move.
    - **B.** The magnets will push apart.
    - **C.** The magnets will pull together.

5. What does the word **levitates** mean in this book?

*So, the train does not touch the tracks. Instead, the train **levitates**.*

   A. travels quickly
   B. stays in the air
   C. touches other things

6. What does the word **clings** mean in this book?

*The magnet **clings** to the refrigerator. It holds the drawing in place.*

   A. sticks
   B. carries
   C. separates

Answer key on page 32.

GLOSSARY

atoms
Tiny units of matter that most of the objects around us are made of.

attracted
Pulled toward.

compass
A tool used to show direction.

electrons
Charged particles that can be in atoms or on their own.

poles
The points where the magnetic field lines enter and leave a magnet.

repel
To push away from.

sanitation
Having to do with removing trash.

TO LEARN MORE

BOOKS

Eboch, Chris. *Magnets in the Real World.* Minneapolis: Abdo Publishing, 2013.

Spilsbury, Louise, and Richard Spilsbury. *Magnetism.* Chicago: Heinemann Library, 2014.

Walker, Sally M. *Investigating Magnetism.* Minneapolis: Lerner Publications, 2012.

NOTE TO EDUCATORS

Visit **www.focusreaders.com** to find lesson plans, activities, links, and other resources related to this title.

INDEX

A
atoms, 14
attract, 7–8, 13, 16, 20

C
compass, 24

E
electrons, 15

I
iron, 11, 13, 15

L
lodestones, 11, 13

M
magnetic field, 13–16, 24

N
nickel, 15

P
poles, 16, 24

R
refrigerators, 5, 7, 19
repel, 8, 16, 22

T
trains, 22–23

Answer Key: 1. Answers will vary; **2.** Answers will vary; **3.** B; **4.** B; **5.** B; **6.** A